STORY OF HER

A Story of Redemption

JULY 5, 2024
ANGELINA BENITEZ
Chicago, Illinois

A huge thank you:

To God for making this possible. Thank you, Jesus, for saving me and helping me see who I was. Praising you all the days of my life. Thank you for being a Father to the fatherless.

To my husband Milton: I love you. Thank you for the endless support and love you show me. I am so grateful that this story ends with you.

To my boys: Isaiah, Angel, Christian, and Joel know that I love you more than anything and am so blessed to have you in my world. I am so glad God chose me to be your mom. I pray that you surround yourself with the love of Jesus.

To my new children: Israel and Kristina I am so happy that I get to be in your lives. You all are a blessing and I love you both. God has so much in store for you.

To my grandmother: Thank you for being there when I needed you, for helping me raise my boys. I love you so much.

Preface

No, in all these things we are more than conquerors through him who loved us.

Romans 8:37

I was in the shower one morning and I was washing my face I began to just cry, this was not the "I am so frustrated" cry, this was a cry of gratitude. I woke up and smiled, I woke up eager to get my day started and ready to get to work. That has not always been the case, I dreaded waking up and what the day was going to bring. I have come a long way, from the girl who did not like who she saw in the mirror, who wanted to hide from the world, which could not provide for her kids to this determined, grateful, and bold woman. I wish I could say it took me a few years to get here, I am forty-two and I have just arrived! I can walk around with my head up high, which sounds so cliché but that is how it is. I love being the light wherever I go. I no longer have the victim mentality, I am no longer a victim, but a Warrior. An overcomer and a conqueror! I am an overcomer because I have victory in Jesus who saved me. Once I realized that my past and what I had been through no longer defined me, a new door opened for me. When I realized who I was in Christ, my life changed. When I was walking around with the "woe is me" attitude, I was unhappy, broke, and mentally drained. So that says a lot. I also surrounded myself with those that had that same attitude and that just made things worse. I had to knock it off, and I did. I just wish I did not take as long as it did. But one thing that I have learned is that everything has a purpose. Everything that we go through is for a purpose. I genuinely believe that. You might not see it while it's happening, but one day I promise you will be like "Dang that's why that happened" I will often get asked "How do you do it" and "Give me some motivation" Here is the thing about that, I can give you all the motivation all day every day, I can tell what to do, I can tell you what works for me but until you are ready for a change none of that will matter. Until you realize that the only way to have a fulfilling life is to give your life to Jesus, He is the way, the truth, and the life. You can hear all the motivational speakers every second of the day, but motivation does not last, we can get excited about something, and we can be that way for a few days, and boom you go back to how it was. I spent my entire life wondering if I would ever be happy, if I would ever heal, would I ever love myself. I now know what was missing this whole time, and I am so grateful to have found it. I thank you in advance for coming along with me on my journey. It was not pretty, nor easy, but I hope that after you are finished reading you realize that no matter the circumstance you can overcome and live the life that is meant for you. Welcome to The Story of Her! A story of hope, a story of redemption.

CHAPTER 1: Memories

You would be surprised at what our mind holds on to. I recall things that happened when I was two, and you are like no way but. I even shocked my mom with the details I had provided to her. Now mind you some say it could have been a dream and argue with me that those are not memories, but I know what I have seen. Let us talk about my mom for a minute, her story is quite important because we all know that cycles repeat themselves and the person my mom is stems from how she was brought up. My mom is the strongest woman I know, I will not go into details because I will respect her privacy. My mom was the oldest of five kids and was not treated the best, she was not hugged and loved like a child should. She was responsible for helping my grandmother with her siblings. She had to learn a lot and she missed her childhood. Having her innocence taken away from enduring pain at an early age resulted in her growing up knowing pain. Again, difficult childhoods lead to difficult adulthoods. I will say that my mother was a teenager looking for love, but not the kind that you are thinking. She was not looking for a man to sweep her off her feet. She did not even trust men, but she was wanting to give all her love to someone and have someone love her unconditionally. Fast forward she did meet someone who became very fond of her, my mom was such a beautiful girl, she caught the attention of all the guys in the neighborhood. She had long, deep brown hair, wore cute clothes and looked older. So long story short, she got with someone, and I was the result. Now it was not all rainbows and roses, she had to deal with a whole lot to have me, but she did. My real father was not the nicest man to my mom and again I will not go into detail but this one memory I have has never left my brain. I cannot even recall what she was wearing, but there I was in my crib, I was about two, and I remember seeing my mom getting dragged across the floor, I remember seeing her hair wrapped around my father's hand. That was the end of the memory. I also remember feeling the love of my father, and my mom confirmed that when she said that he would make sure I ate, and he treated me like a princess. Feeling the love of a father quickly ended when he said that he was going to go to the store to get me candy and never came back. I never saw him again until I was about ten and that was for five minutes, what is so crazy is I have no recollection of what he looked like. After that it was just me and momma, she struggled to feed herself but always made sure to feed me. Also, I was so extra and sensitive that I could not wear normal diapers like any other kids so my mom would have to wash my cloth diapers in the toilet every night and all day. There was a neighbor who befriended my mom and would feed us, she later became a huge part of our lives. My biological father did return but I did not see him, he decided to have his way and impregnated my mom two more times before he was gone. So, you see my mom has endured a lot, and that is not even the end or half of it. Our memory is funny because my mind goes back to me being five and my mom having my baby sister. I remember when she was born, I thought she

was a doll and I just wanted to hold her all the time. We lived in an apartment on

the South Side of Chicago that was not the best, we had rodents that looked like

cats and many times we did not have electricity. At that time, I had no idea what

was going on, I did not know it was a struggle. Suddenly, my mom was about to

have her fourth child, my baby sister. I remember my mom being sick and could

not get out of bed, so I quickly learned how to feed a baby. I loved my baby sister

so much that I used to tell her to call me mommy. I can remember my sister

Vanessa being the one who was always in trouble, and my brother Pedro was

always just there, playing with his toys. That was my world and I loved them. I

remember days when we would go into the fridge and eat margarine from the tub

because we were hungry, my mother still cries about that to this day. But the

struggle was real for her. She did not have anyone. It was just us. I can remember

my aunt Delia being there, but she was a young teenager as well, so I do not recall

a lot of her time there. But I could have just blocked out a lot from that time. Once

we got a bit older, I remember us moving to a different apartment in the Back of

the Yards neighborhood; this time my two aunts were living with us. I can

remember them having a fun time while we were running around like crazy kids.

We had a great uncle who was a Firefighter and one day he brought over a bicycle,

I was already too afraid to learn how to ride it. My brother, Pedro, was determined to learn; we had this huge yard in front of our apartment building, and he went out there, got on the bike, held on to the fence, and pushed until he finally learned. My brother was always the athletic type, I remember him always getting hurt from playing sports in school. Basketball was his favorite. I can remember the smell of my mom making breakfast in the mornings, and us all sleeping on the same bed. I remember my mom working several jobs to make ends meet and walking home late at night from my grandmother's house. My mom did the best that she could to provide for us. We faced many trials, my mother went through a lot and one of my favorite memories is that she would sing this song to me, it was called "You and Me against the World" by Helen Reddy. At the time I did not know what the song meant I just knew that every time she sang it to me, she would cry. I remember watching her comb her hair in the bathroom and thinking she was the prettiest mom in the world. Now I do not recall many birthdays from my childhood, but when I was seven my mom gave me a party and I remember having fun. My best friend at the time, Katrina, was there. Katrina and I were friends for many years then she moved. I reconnected with her years later, but people often drift away. One of the things that I remember was us making our tie-dyed shirts, now do not laugh that style was in! We would fill the kitchen sink and add all our colors, it was the best. If that kitchen sink could talk it would tell you how many times my mom had to wash our clothes in it. I can see her now with the scrubbing board and her scrubbing away. She always did what she had to do; she is who I learned from. And all that I am is because of my mom. One of the things I can also remember is my mom had to work a lot and did not have anyone to watch us, you see so it was just me and her against the world. At that time, I had no idea what was in store for us as a family, as teenagers, and as adults. Life does not come with a rule book and none of us are exempt from facing challenges. I was a little girl, who was about to encounter not-so-little things that would forever leave impressions on my soul. Some good and some bad. I am very vocal about my situations and challenges for one main purpose, and you will find out why.

Chapter Two: Stolen Innocence

This may be the hardest chapter for me to write, but it is part of my story, and I will always be transparent and honest with my journey. It is a part of me and what makes Angelina the resilient woman you see today. It shows how much Jesus has healed me from the inside. We often hear the phrase "my innocence was taken" and most of us can get an idea of what that means. If one has never experienced this, it may be hard to understand why this takes such a toll on your spirit and adult life. I have heard so many times, "Oh you will have to get over it, or it was so long ago just forget about it." The fact of the matter is I will never forget what happened, but I have forgiven the individuals responsible so that I can be at peace with it. I have accepted that those incidents are part of my story, I share them with you all because I pray that someone can use my experience and begin to heal and learn that those circumstances do not define you nor do they control you. So here it is.

We lived in this apartment in the Back of the Yards neighborhood, it was not the biggest place, but it was our place. My siblings and I shared a room, we had bunk beds, so my brother slept on top, and my sister and I shared the bottom bunk. My mom had this good friend who spent a lot of time with us. She had a brother who also would come over and hang out with us. We were all comfortable around them. I was seven at the time and all I remember is that I would smile when they were there. On this random night, my baby sister got a high fever and my mom had to take her to the hospital. My mom did not want to leave us alone, so she called her friend. The friend's brother had to stay with us. I remember her coming into the room and mentioning that he was going to watch us. We were well-behaved kids, so she knew that we would not give him any trouble. It was also bedtime, so we started getting ready for bed and Mom left. I wish she had not. Here we were in the dark and we were typical kids who never went right to bed, we were laughing, and I remember him coming into the room and telling us to be quiet. It was different this time. I felt scared and I never felt that way with him. It is so crazy to me how I can recall every detail from that night. I was seven! A normal seven-year-old little girl. I had no idea that the events from that night would be the root cause of so many of my issues growing up. I do not know how much time has passed, but I am still awake, and I see the door opening, he walks in, and my heart starts beating fast. Now at the time, I did not know what I was supposed to be afraid of. Also, I am telling this story through the eyes of a little girl who had no idea what was happening. He was a big man; he was a chubby man with messy hair and the palest skin I had seen. There he is sitting on my bed; I am pretending that I am sleeping. "Wake up" I hear him say so I open my eyes and his face is so close to mine. I can smell his breath. I did not like that feeling that I had at that very moment. I was sleeping on my side, and he told me to lay on my stomach, I hesitated to do what he said. That made him mad, he told me "If you don't then I will get your sister" I do not know what happened, but I immediately felt protective and turned over on my stomach. My little sister was asleep on her side facing the wall. He started to pull down my pajama pants, I was laying there, and it was like I was frozen. He then climbed on top and suddenly, I was in between his legs. I turned around and he pushed my face back into the pillow and said, "Stay still," his tone was so scary to me. He said that I needed to listen to him, or he was going to hurt my sister. I did not move; I did what he said. I feel his hands on my rear end, he begins rubbing me and touching my back. What happens next is disturbing and will be difficult to read but again, you must understand exactly what happened. I immediately feel something hard and then I feel it in between my buttocks. I did not know what was going on, and I did not even know what to do. I just knew I was scared, I yelled because it was hurting, and he told me to be quiet. Tears fell down my cheek and I squeezed my eyes closed. The next few minutes seemed to last forever. After what seemed like an eternity, I felt a wet liquid all over me and then he got off me and reminded me to never tell my mother what just happened. After he left my room, I just lay there and could not move. I lay there crying and wanting my mom. I was afraid to go to the bathroom, so I took a shirt from my bag of dirty clothes, wiped myself off, and climbed back into bed. I hugged my sister and cried to myself to sleep. I had no idea that what happened that night would have been the beginning of my struggles. I would go on keeping this a secret until I was thirteen or so.

As I look back, I always wonder if that person knew what he did to my soul, to my spirit. I am sure I was not the first or the last one to have experienced him. Did he care that he had me so scared; I was seven years old. A little girl that smiled and that day she lost it. Little did I know that was only the beginning of feeling that way. It only adds right the other incidents in this chapter as well. My grandmother would go to Mexico every year with her husband, the man that I knew as Grandpa. She would take care of her grandkids with her, and we would be gone for six weeks. I remember the first time I went; we drove there, and Grandpa had a station wagon. I remember the drive lasting forever and stopping to use the restrooms. This one time someone joined us to help Grandfather drive, so I was in the backseat and Grandpa was also in the backseat, he was lying on my lap and covered in a blanket. I was a little girl and did not know that he was as demented as the man I dealt with when I was seven. All I know is that I was sleeping, and I felt hands on my legs, and then he put his easily my pants, I tried to push his hand away, but he did it harder. I was scared and just stood still. He stuck his fingers in me and decided to violate that grandfather/granddaughter relationship. He did not stop there, we arrived at a hotel after driving for a while, I was sleeping in my bed, and Grandma was taking a shower. Suddenly, someone sits on my bed, I am afraid to even open my eyes and seconds later his hands are all over me again. He had decided that he was going to touch me how he wanted to. I was helpless. Suddenly, the water turned off in the shower and he took his hands off me and jumped off my bed. I spent the rest of the trip trying to forget that. I dreaded going to sleep every night, I was scared that every time my grandmother was not around, he would try again. These men had decided to take a piece of my innocence and I would deal with the consequences for most of my childhood, teenage, and adulthood. At this point, I am wondering if this is normal, I could not trust any men. There are so many emotions that go along with being abused in that way. The feeling of fear, the feeling of shame, and anger all at the same time. You go through life feeling dirty and like it was your fault. I remember the day that I told my mother what had happened when I was seven. It was only because of what happened to my grandfather that all those feelings came back, and I had to let them out. We were in the kitchen, and I told her, and she fell to the floor. See my mom did not want history to repeat itself and she just found out that it did. She fell to the floor, and she called the police, but they made it clear that there was nothing that could be done since so much time had passed. Years later the sight of seeing that man's sister would take me back to that scared little girl.

Chapter 3: High School Years.

You always hear people say that high school is the best time of your life. Well, I

loved it so much that I decided to stay an extra year. No, that was not my intention

but there are always consequences for your actions. I went into high school scared

and excited at the same time, I was such a shy teenager and awkward too. I was

trying to not be seen and was very insecure in myself. My wardrobe consisted of

boss jeans and an oversized T-shirt, because I was a chubby teenager, I figured I

was hiding all my flaws with bigger clothes. If there was a scent that describes my

high school years it would be Cucumber Melon, which was my favorite body

spray. I remember my first day of school, I was so afraid that I would get made fun

of, I had friends in grammar school that would get teased and called names. I spent

some of my first year of high school living at my grandmother's house. Being the

oldest, I had a lot of responsibility, so my being there ensured that I could focus on

school and get adjusted to the transition. I would wake up super early and make

sure I looked and smelled good. Then my grandma would have breakfast ready for

me, it was usually 2 sunny-side-up eggs, bacon, and a couple of tortillas. I did not

do any chores; I would come home and get right to my homework. We did that for

half the year and then I went back home. By the time I got to my sophomore year, I

was not as shy, I started looking for clubs to join and had a sizable number of

friends. I was still dressing in boy's clothes, but that did not end until my junior year. Junior year is the year things changed, I began liking boys, and I started working at this fast-food place. I was exposed to a whole new world. I had my very first boyfriend there. We did not end up working out, and that was ok. I do not know how, but I fit right in. I will never forget my crew. I enjoyed that job, my coworkers ended up being my close friends and helped me come out of my shell. I started wearing makeup, wearing tighter clothes.

I was beginning to experience the world and its worldly ways. I also remember getting into so much trouble while being at that place, my mom was not happy with some of my behavior. You know it was a fast-food place and it required me to stay late and come home late. I did have to deal with the consequences like getting up late for school and missing my 1st and 2nd period classes. Many times, the guy that I had crushing on would bring me home and we would take our sweet time, I will never forget us driving up to my house and my mom being outside furious! At that time, I was simply going with the flow, I liked him, so I wanted to spend a lot of time with him, even if it got me in trouble. Let us just say I started getting a bit braver and just feeling myself. I was getting older, I was rebelling.

I remember one day being at work and my crush asked me if I wanted to go to the movies with him. I was so freaking excited. I told my mom and even though I was acting like a jerk she permitted me to go. The only thing was that my stepdad was very old-fashioned and did not want me to date anyone. We produced a plan, and I spent the weekend with my grandma, and he picked me up from there. Here we are watching this typical chick flick, which was about high school life, it was my first real date! I was so nervous but comfortable at the same time. He was becoming my best friend. He was a year older than me and went to another high school. Right before he dropped me off at my grandmother's house, he asked me if I would go to the prom with him. Can you imagine how I felt? Out of all the girls in his school, he wanted me to go to his senior prom with him! I immediately said of course and went in and told my grandma the whole story. I went to his prom and had the time of my life. I remember thinking that this was what I had to look forward to. I would be a happy young adult; I would have tons of friends and go off to college and be a child psychologist. All that came to my mind as we were dancing to "Sweet Lady" by Tyrese.

 Before I knew it Senior year was here. I was not doing a particularly decent job of keeping up with my schoolwork. And it was catching up to me, I was cutting class and not turning in assignments. This year I slacked off, and the thing is I have no idea why. I had a lot of friends; I was in clubs and for some reason, I still wanted to do my own thing. This one time my friends and I decided to ditch and go to our bestie's house because it was her birthday. Well, her older brother was there, and he decided to get us all drunk. And I am not talking about giving us wine coolers or beer, this man was giving us shots of tequila and rum. It is safe to say that it did not end well. But it was a lesson learned and did I pay! Graduation season arrived and I was told that I will not be walking down the aisle with my friends. To be honest, I was ok with that, but I was afraid to tell my mom. So much so that I developed a tension ball of some sort on my neck. But I needed to accept that I goofed off. I was not ready to be out in the real world, I wonder if I subconsciously tried to stall that process. I was not going to graduate on stage, I would have to go to school until January to get all my credits. I accepted that I had no choice. My baby sister was starting high school that year. We made the most of it, I ate lunch with her and her friends. Suddenly, I had all these "baby sisters." I went to the classes that I needed to attend and had fun for the rest of the day. When January came, I decided to just stay, I did not want to leave that school for some reason. It was like I felt so safe there. And it was not like my home life was bad, I just felt secure within those school walls. Now I am not proud of my actions that led to my five-year plan, but I cannot change it. It is a part of my story. I mean, I got to go to extra proms as well which is nothing to brag about, but I had the time of my life. I made so many memories during my high school years, good and bad. I remember the body spray I used to use, the food I ate, picking up my best friend, and walking together while drooling over our crushes. I remember my favorite biology teacher and counselor who believed that I could be anything I wanted to be. I carry so many things with me from those years, and they will stay with me forever. I recall being obsessed with Herbal Essence products, and pear scented body sprays. I remember the girls that I wanted to be like. You know the perfect girls with the best bodies and beautiful hair. I spent my entire high school life wanting to be someone else. I wanted to be the girl that had a lot of guys crushing on her, I wanted to be president of the student council and be the funny girl everyone loved being around. I was not satisfied; I was constantly looking for fulfillment and validation. This behavior would continue and rollover into my adult life.

Chapter 4: My firstborn.

There was a time in my life when I did not want kids. I was the oldest of five and knew what it was like to care for a child. But then it shifted, and I could not wait to have a daughter. If you had told me that I was going to be a "Boy Mom" I would have never believed you. Here I am 22 years old and celebrating the New Year with my partner at the time and his sister who was also my best friend. There I crouched over in front of our Round Lake home. All I saw was all the blue drinks that I consumed that night. The next day my friend asked if I had gotten my period yet, I told her no but that it was all over the place since I got on the pill. I just thought it was normal. I remember her saying that I needed to take a test and I looked at her angrily and said, "girl you are crazy!" Finally, she convinced me to take a test a couple of days later, so I went to the bathroom and peed on the stick. I remember being so scared, seconds later the 2 pink lines showed up. I was in shock! I mean the whole point of birth control was to not get pregnant, and here I have this test and it is saying that I am going to be a MOM! I stood in the bathroom and cried for an hour; I was not ready to be a mom. Yes, I knew what it was like to take care of kids, but I did not want that yet. Subconsciously I knew that my partner and I would not last, and I was going to end up being a single mom. There was no love in that relationship. After calming down I decided to embrace it, I was going to be a mom. I will be a great mom I kept thinking. I was babysitting my nephew at the time and loved washing his clothes and folding his little laundry, so

I was looking forward to all those things. I must tell you that this is all going on in

my head as I am in the bathroom. I finally decided to surprise my partner and turn

the test into a gift, but I did not get the reaction I expected, all my joy and

happiness went out the window. He was not happy and showed it. I was mortified,

I felt stuck. My family was far from me, and I felt so alone.

My first pregnancy was not an easy one by any means, I was sick every day,

and I was losing weight instead of gaining. My doctor gave me medication to at

least be able to keep some food down and I was obsessed with McDonald's

chicken sandwiches. My partner was not working at the time, so it was tough, Now

I will not bash him, but I felt more alone than ever before. He was not showing any

empathy or even love during this time. My best friend and her BF at the time made

sure that I ate every day, they would get me all the things I was craving and just

took care of me. I will forever be thankful to them both. One of my favorite movies

at that time was "Losing Isaiah" We were watching it one day and I decided that is

what I would name my baby boy. I started planning and preparing for the arrival of

my baby boy and loved that idea more. All I cared about was him, my partner

made it clear I was in this by myself with his actions. Here we are nine months

later, and it looks like I am still not ready, so the plan is to induce labor in two

weeks if it does not happen on its own. So, my baby decided that he wanted to continue being in my belly so off to the hospital I went to get induced. All I remember is me crying on the phone with my grandmother, I was so scared. She was on the phone trying to calm me down and reminding me that I did not want to get an epidural. I would clutch the bed rails and the pain was the worst that I had ever felt. My partner at some point showed up and was sitting on the chair being anything but a comfort to me. After the doctor said that I may not deliver until the morning, he got up and left. I wanted to scream at that time because I expected him to want to stay with me. As soon as he left the nurse came to check to see how I was, and it turns out baby Isaiah was coming. My son was entering the world, and I was alone. The nurse called my partner and left a message to come back, but he missed it. I will never forget that day and seeing my baby boy for the first time. I was a mom, my baby whom I had carried for 9 months was finally in my arms. He was so small and looked like a little old man! He was wrinkly and had no hair and looked at him as if he were angry, but he was so beautiful to me.

Isaiah was my new reason to live. I adored him. Isaiah was in a different outfit every day and I would take a picture daily. I would hold him and tell him I would be the best mom ever. I made it a point to break these generational curses, but they were mere words then. I had no idea how I would do that. I just wanted to protect him. Isaiah is now 20 years old; I cannot believe how much time has passed. He is full of goodness and not afraid to go after what he wants. I could not have asked for a better son. He has been through trials and is working toward healing and being the man that God intended him to be. He did not let our circumstances and trials make him bitter and have a hardened heart. He is kind, and he is loved wherever he goes. I cannot wait to see what God does with him and how he will use his past trauma to impact others. I know most people say that you should not be friends with your kids but let me tell you, my son has been my right hand, and I cannot imagine my life without him. I love that he can come to me and discuss the most awkward situations, I will always be here to listen and guide him. He has moved out of our home, and I pray God keep his hand on Him and his life.

Chapter 5: Angel Xavier

I remember the day I decided I wanted to go back to Chicago, I needed to be around my family. I wanted to get that connection back with my mom, there was an apartment that was for rent downstairs from her. I convinced my partner to move us to Chicago. I was also thinking that if we ended up splitting up then at least I would have my family there. I knew that I would not be growing old with this man. Even before I had put all my faith in my God, I knew this was not part of the plan. There was no love, no compassion and I felt completely alone. No matter what, he still came home to a hot meal at the table and his house cleaned but we were not even around each other anymore. The minute he came home from work, Isaiah and I would go upstairs to my mom's. We were not intimate anymore; it was only a matter of time before we split up. I was not happy and certainly not in love with him. I had reconnected with a school friend of mine, and she would come over and we would sit outside of my place and just catch up. One day she brought her boyfriend and another guy. He immediately caught my attention, but I brushed it off. She introduced me to him, and I was intrigued, he was very mysterious and looked like 50 cent! I did not think much of it, and I certainly did not imagine what would happen. Now this is not one of my proudest moments because at the end of the day, I was still living with my partner. I was confused because this guy had my interest, and I knew I had his. I knew it would not be anything serious because he did not live in Chicago, he was just visiting. We went on a few dates, and I found myself having feelings for him. To be honest those were feelings of being wanted. I was not getting that at home. This in no way excused the fact that this was wrong. I ended up sleeping with this man, and he knew all the things he wanted to say to have me in awe.

I thought this could be the beginning of a good relationship. I thought I finally found my knight in shining armor.

 One night my partner and I went to a party, and I was drinking, we got home and all I remember was waking up the next morning naked. I was confused because we had not been sleeping together in months, we were growing apart. I was mad and I yelled and told him that He had taken advantage of me because I was drunk. We went back to our normal routine, barely speaking. Weeks went by and I realized that my cycle was late, I was starting to feel sick, and I immediately got so scared! Am I pregnant, I thought! I started thinking about the timeline of when my partner and I had sex and when I had sex with K. I was desperate, I was convinced it was my partner's because I used protection with K. I had to tell K though, he came, and stood outside my gate, and I told him I was pregnant. I did not know what type of response I was hoping to get. He looked me in the eye and said, "Get rid of it" and walked away. That was the last time I had seen him.

There I was on the stairs watching him walk away from me. I felt completely lost and scared. At that time, it seemed normal for girls to get pregnant, and go to the clinic to "take care of it" I asked my best friend at the time where she went, and I remember calling the place and they were so rude. I immediately hung up and cried it out. I had no idea what I was going to do. Dark thoughts filled my head. There I was one day sitting in the living room, looking at Isaiah, and thinking "How am I going to raise 2 babies" I called the place that my friend recommended. It was an abortion clinic on the North Side of Chicago. The woman who answered was so rude that I immediately hung up. I grabbed the phone book, which was a huge yellow book with every business you could think of. It was the "Google" of that time. I found this place that was near to me and called to make an appointment. The lady was sweet, and I felt some type of comfort. I went that day with my heart pounding, I was scared. I did not want to be there. I remember sitting in this office and a woman showed up, her energy was so soothing. I cannot explain it. She had the sweetest voice and asked me a few questions. She said that she needed to show me a video about the procedure so that I knew what was about to happen. Minutes later I am there watching this horrific video! I could not believe what was about to happen. I began to cry and then she walked in. She sat in her chair and said "Sweety why are you here?" I cried and expressed that I could not raise these two kids, I was not financially stable, and I would be alone. As I am weeping, I hear her say, "What if we help you with clothing, formula, and diapers, you know all the things that you need?" I looked up at her and cried "Really?" I continued to weep, she then handed me a booklet of vouchers and instructed me to go to the 1st floor and shop for maternity clothing. I will never forget her. I went home that day and was upset at what I did. I went on with life. Nine months went by so fast, Angel was two weeks late, so I had to get induced. I went in and had my baby. He was an angel, he was so perfect, all I could do was cry. My aunt had paid for baby pictures of Angel when he was born, I had sent one along with a Thank you card to Mary at the Center. For a year they provided me with clothing, diapers, walkers, and formula. I will forever be thankful to her and what she did for me. She was one of the many angels that God had sent to me. Angel would grow up to be a child that has shown resilience. Like Isaiah, he also faced many trials due to our circumstances. There would be childhood trauma and mental health issues with which he would deal. He would also be my prodigal son. My biggest prayer is that God will call him and that he will have an encounter with Jesus. That his heart would be softened, and he would know that true restoration comes from accepting Jesus into your heart. My God is big, I believe that Angel will be transformed by the blood of Jesus and serve right alongside my husband and me.

Chapter 6: Searching

Being a mom of two boys was quite an adventure. After my son Angel was born, I dealt with postpartum depression. Things were still not going well with my partner. He decided that Angel was his child no matter what happened. I thought that was very noble of him, so we tried to make it work. It did not work, if anything it got worse. My grandmother would come over to my house every morning and help me with the boys. I was so thankful, I felt so depressed though. The next eight months were a blur and resulted in the final and official breakup of my partner and me. It was a long time coming. I went to live with my mom and brother.

My mom worked at a nursing home and said we could stay and get things situated. We slept out in the living room, and I tried looking for work. Angel was not even a year yet and Isaiah was almost two years old. It was such a weird time. I was not sure what I was feeling, but I was struggling, struggling to buy diapers, and stressed. I remember every week I would try to gather twenty-five dollars for diapers. I would even use a T-shirt as a diaper. I felt like a failure. I needed a job, but I could not afford a daycare and had nobody who could watch my babies. My mom worked full time and so did my brother. I began doing what any lost person does and started seeking attention and love. I was still this broken child now forced to be a grown-up with children and not knowing what I was doing. I was craving love and guidance but from the wrong places. I became consumed by all the wrong things.

I began chatting with people through a dating app, and I filled my time with meaningless conversations, demanding requests, and empty promises. I was the typical girl who grew up with daddy issues looking for love and found everything but that. I started going out late at night, meeting up with guys, and being reckless. My brother and mom would come home from work and then I would leave the kids with them. I wanted to be loved and accepted so I did anything these men asked. It was not long before I came across someone who would make me feel secure and safe, but he was feeding off my insecurities. He preyed on me, and I did not see it at first. I gave my all to please him and not make him upset. Looking back at the red flags that were there from the very beginning, I ignored them all. The next couple of years were filled with tears, mixed emotions, and confusion. Where was God? Why did I end up this way? Why couldn't I be happy? Did I not deserve that? These were the questions I asked myself over and over. For a long time, I wished that I had not met this person, and now I see the purpose. I had to go through it, no matter how much it hurt.

Chapter 7: The Abortion

Here we are 4 years into this relationship, I say we because I have my two sons. By this time, my kids and I had moved in with my grandmother. My grandma had this big house, and she loved my boys. I found out that I was pregnant, and I was happy because I thought it would change him, I thought he would take care of us. I just thought all the wrong things. Once he found out, he was mad. He said we would not have the baby. I told him I would have it and did not need him to stay with me. I was afraid of him, what he said was law. I had no say, I had no voice.

 One day he picked me up and drove me to a clinic. I cried and asked him to just take me home. Nothing worked, I was in that place. I felt like I wanted to throw up, I wanted someone to help me. I thought about telling someone that he was making me do this. But the fear of the consequences would not allow me to. This was happening, I already knew what the process was and for that, I was even more upset. I go back to the room and cannot contain the tears. I did not want to be there. I made up scenarios in my head about escaping. It seemed like an eternity being in that waiting room when I heard my name. I hoped someone would ask me why I was crying, but I am sure they have seen many crying faces.

They told me to get undressed and put the hospital gown on, I lay on the bed and the next thing I remember was waking up and I asked where my baby was. Nobody answered me at first. I started to cry, and the nurse began to rub my head and tried to calm me down. I told her, "I know my baby was a girl" "It does not matter now, you are ok" the nurse responded. But I was not ok.

I felt like a piece of me died that day. I walked out of that place empty. I did not care what he did to me. I could not say a word the whole car ride. "If God wanted us to have a baby, then he wouldn't have let this happen" is what my partner would tell me. I believed him for a while, but that still did not take away the grief. For years he would continue to tell me that. I would blame him and blame myself for what I did. My baby would have been born sometime around October. For years to come, I would mourn my baby. Mourn the loss. I made it clear that I would never forgive him for what he made me do. He did not care, he was cold. He did not have to go through the process or feel. I was alone in this.

Chapter 8: Christian

Another year in this relationship and at this point I just wanted out. We were not happy; my kids were afraid of him, and I could not break away from him. I was his property; I know he did not love me. This was possession at its finest. We got another surprise when I found out that I was pregnant. I cried out to God asking why!!?? What if he made me abort again? I could not bear that. At this point, God was like all the men in my life who had hurt me, so I had a problem with God. I was mad at him because of everything that was happening to me and my kids. This time when I told this man that I was pregnant, he was happy. I was so confused, just a year ago he made me have an abortion and now he is happy that we are having a baby. I was thinking that maybe since he was happy, he would be nicer to us. Perhaps we would go live with him now, but he was not having that. My pregnancy was not the best, I was stressed for most of it. Nine months flew by, and it was all a blur. I always thought a pregnant woman would be spoiled and loved, I cried most of my pregnancy. The baby was two weeks late, so I had to get induced. This labor was tough, my grandmother was there, and my partner was coming and going since he was working. I had the baby, and my grandmother was the first to hold him, my Christian was here. He was so beautiful; He had so much dark hair and my grandma fell in love with him. I was so happy that he was here. But at the same time sad because of the situation, he was born in. I loved my baby so much.

Isaiah and Angel loved being his big brothers. We continued to live at my grandmother's house, and she would watch the kids as I began to look for work. My grandmother and Christian had a special bond, and it continues to this day. Christian is now thirteen and I cannot imagine my life without him. He has such a big heart despite all we have been through. He can make anything out of cardboard, and I have to say that my heart melts every time I see him smile. Like his brothers, he has faced sadness, but He now belongs to Jesus!

Chapter 9: Then there was Joel.

Here comes my baby! There was so much that happened before I had Joel. We are about seven years into this relationship and now I am having another baby. Still stressed, still unhappy, and looking for a way out. This was life to me at this point. By this time we had already moved out of my grandmother's house. We lived about 15 minutes from her place. I could not believe I was having another baby, again I questioned God because I was like "God you see what we are going through, why do you keep letting this happen." Joel was being difficult at the end of the pregnancy. He kept turning in the womb, so they had to do a C-section. He was two weeks late just like the other boys. That was such a weird experience, it did not hurt because of the pain meds but I could feel all the tugging and pulling. Finally, He was here, and he was a chunky baby, his cheeks were so cute, and I loved him the moment I saw him. Joel would grow up to be the cutest toddler in my eyes, his skin was fair, he had light brown curly hair, the cutest nose, and a smile that melted everyone's heart. Whenever I was sad or felt depressed, I would look at his face and I could not help but smile. I was a stay-at-home mom when we had Joel, I saw all the milestones, and he was the ultimate momma's boy.

One of the things that I am grateful for is that Joel was the youngest, so he did not comprehend what was happening at home. He does not seem to have any memories; I am glad he remains an innocent child. He is a normal ten-year-old fourth grader who prefers to not go to school and watch YouTube all day. He loves to be the center of attention and will tell the same joke twenty times until he gets acknowledged. I love that he asks so many questions and is a funny kid. I am grateful that the Lord chose me to be his mom. I love watching him grow up, I love that he has this version of me. The after-Christ version of Mom. I cannot wait to see what the Lord has in store for him.

Chapter 10-My First Encounter.

Let us go back a little bit to my first marriage. Joel was a year old when his dad and I got married. We had been together for 9 years. I cannot sit here and say that I was happy because God knows I was not. You must understand my frame of mind during this time, I felt stuck, I was depressed, I was eating away my feelings, and I wanted to sleep all the time. I was not happy. But I did not know how to get away from it. I could not escape him. I was still afraid of him and since I did not work, he would say I needed him. You start to believe all the lies you get told, so I was just trying to survive, I would put on the happy face and the 'happy family' pictures for Facebook. But it was all fake. I wanted out. I took it and took it until one day it was enough. Part of my testimony is that I encountered Jesus for the first time on that night.

After an argument that night with my partner I was on the floor and was trying to catch my breath, I wanted it to just be over. I was tired. I wanted to go to sleep and not wake up. I am laying there and suddenly, I hear "Get up, you're ok" I got up and cleaned myself up. At that moment I did not know what to think of it. Was it God?

Something happened inside me that day, I had my mind made up, I was leaving that place. I began to plan. I had no money, and no car. I did not care, I left that place two weeks later. I did not care what it took, I grabbed out clothes and some

paperwork and never went back. I wish I could say that it ended peacefully, but the

next three years were unbearable, or so it seemed. My boys and I moved right back

to my grandmother's house. I began working and trying to provide for my kids.

We struggled, but I was not alone. My grandma helped so much and was there

when we needed her. I will forever us this as part of my story, Jesus had been with

me the whole time, I just did not see it.

Chapter 11: When the seed was planted.

Let us go back a little bit. I remember going through life thinking that everyone could see my issues, I felt like they could see all the things that I had been through. When we were younger, we would go to church sometimes. We were in the CCD classes, went on Palm Sunday, and did things of the Catholic upbringing. We said, "Our Father" and the "Hail Mary" and that was it. My mom would send us to church on Sunday morning and we would skip and go to our cousin's house! Not our finest moments but we were teenagers. We did not want to be in Church. We would practice lent and give up meat and something like junk food, and that meant that we loved God. Whenever we passed a church, we would do the sign of the cross and wear all the crucifixions. We would go to confession and confess our sins to the priest; he would tell us what to pray and then boom we were forgiven. There I go reciting the 'Our Father' prayer and thinking that was enough. I had no idea what it meant to have a relationship with Jesus Christ. I did not know that I could cry out to Him and lay all my fears, all my shame at his feet. I had no idea that He loved me the way He did. Every man that I thought was there to protect and love me disappointed me, hurt me, abandoned me. This is why I ran from God all those years. I associated Him with a man. I remember the first time my best friend invited me to church. She was attending a non-denominational Christian church. I remember the first worship song she sent me; it was a beautiful melody in

Spanish. It described the worthiness of God. I listened to it nonstop. I had no idea what that meant. I went with my bestie to her church, and it was beautiful. I found a location that was closer to me. I walked into this church, there were so many people. I could not believe that I went by myself. That was out of my comfort zone, yet I immediately felt like I belonged there. I see everyone worship and the pastor preached an amazing and relatable message. I began to feel the tug. I started attending every week and started taking Isaiah and Angel, I did not talk to anyone though. I sat in the back and left as soon as it was over. I stopped going to this church, I spent the next 5 years not attending any church. But my father knew that I would return, it was as if he was waiting for me.

 Let us fast forward to 8 years later, I went back to this church! I knew that was the place I needed to be. I began taking classes to get baptized. I wanted to be reborn again, I wanted to express my love for Jesus. I wanted to give my life to Christ. But how?? I began my lukewarm walk with Christ, but I was not on fire for God or the Word. I did not have any direction or accountability. I backslid and began doing all the things that I was doing before. This meant more meaningless conversations, more drinking, more sexual immorality, and smoking. I was isolating myself and I was not reading the word of God. I remember I would pick up the bible and not understand what I was reading. I still did not belong to my Jesus. I was still feeling the need to belong, I was still looking for ways to numb any pain I had. Although I knew the things I was doing were not of God, I would feel the conviction, yet I was not strong enough to do something about it. I would try to justify what I was doing with the fact that I was a good person with a good heart. I was trying to do it all on my own, I was relying on my strength and trying to be my motivation. Yet I kept disappointing myself and people kept doing it too. I was not delivered from the depression, the anxiety, the need to feel wanted, or the sexual desires. I would lay in bed and think "When am going to be truly happy?" I had a job that I was grateful for, a roof over my head, I was able to provide for my kids and we were in a safe environment. Yet, I was not satisfied. The minute the kids left the house I would just cry, I would listen to sad music, and drink the night away. It was not the life I wanted for myself, and at that point, I did not know what it would look like. I was lost, looking to the world for satisfaction, for love and acceptance.

Looking back there were so many areas of my life that needed to be redeemed. I had little patience; I was full of pride. I would motivate others but the minute the camera was off I went back to the little girl that felt so abandoned. I would constantly have these bad memories that I would harp on, I would try to figure out why things happened the way that they did. I longed for validation from others. I would post a picture on social media the minute I needed a boost. I would have many conversations with men just to make me smile for a few moments.

All of that created temporary feelings, inside I was broken and needed salvation. I needed to be redeemed. I wondered if God was punishing me. That sounds so absurd to me now even as I type this. But it was my mentality back then. God had 10% of me and the world had the other 90%. God calls us to be set apart from this world. We are to be a light among the darkness that surrounds the world. I was a part of that darkness. No wonder I was feeling the way that I was. I lost hope, my faith was hanging on by a thread and I was out of control. They often say that a breakdown indicates that there will be a breakthrough. I would go to church and wish I had what everyone else had, I did not know how to get it. I often tell my best friend how grateful I am that she invited me to church, that she shared worship music with me, that she had planted that seed, that the Lord watered it, and it took a decade to see it grow. Although I left, He knew that I would be back home.

Chapter 12: Opportunities.

Once I moved in with my grandmother, I started looking for a job. I heard that there was this Italian place on the north side of Chicago that was hiring. It was a 2-hour bus ride and I hardly seen the kids, but I had a job. The owner was so great and taught me so much about catering and running a business. I was there for almost 2 years and in that time was promoted to Manager and baker. I wore many hats but being a part-time manager was not ideal. I needed something that was full time.

One day my best friend texted me and told me that I should apply where she worked. I thought "sis you are crazy" You see she worked at a huge nonprofit; it is the biggest food pantry in all of Illinois. I turned her down every time she mentioned it. I did not handle rejection very well and I was sure I did not stand a chance. My girl did not give in that easily, she would text me daily asking if I did my resume so I could submit it. I made excuses daily, until one day I was like ok I am just going to apply. I completed the application and then submitted the resume. My resume was not impressive and nothing on there would help me do this job.

You can imagine my surprise when I got a call for an interview, I was shocked and so nervous. What do I wear? What do I say? After completing the first interview a week later I got another call for a second interview. I am in awe! Fast forward to two weeks later, one week before Christmas, I get a call to offer me the position.

Of course, I cried, I was going to be working at a well-known organization,

working in an office, not having to do manual labor, and I could support my kids

and help my grandmother. I was extremely grateful; I remember thinking this was

God. On paper, it did not make sense, but that is where he placed me.

I worked at this organization for four years. I learned and grew so much there.

When I started there, I was quiet and second-guessed everything I did. I was

intimidated by all my colleagues; they all went to college and were smart. But

when I left, I was a lot more confident when it came to my work. I looked forward

to dressing up in business casual clothes every day. My public speaking was so

much better. I was thriving in that position, and then COVID happened. I was

grateful I had a job; we all had to work remotely. That was a challenge, but still,

we got it done.

 Things started to open back up and we returned to the office. I was on the bus one

day and my girl text me and said that I should apply for this nonprofit management

position. I looked at the description and thought, "I have no chance, but I am still

going to apply" By this time, I had learned so much about nonprofits, I figured I

had nothing to lose. You can guess that I got that job, I remember when I had my

interviews and my boss said we need your sunshine and light. I could not believe

it; on paper, I had no business applying for this position, but the Lord opened this door. He really was being so good to me. I was getting a salary; I was making more than I ever imagined. Since being in this position I have had so many opportunities, I am no longer that timid Angelina that gets intimidated with degrees and wealthy ppl. I have been here at this organization for over 2 years now. I have a voice here. I vowed to stay here until the Lord decides to place me elsewhere.

Chapter 13: Starting over.

One year before I started this new job, I decided it was time to move out of my grandmother's house. We had been there longer than I thought. The environment became toxic, not because of my grandmother. That was my girl, but other factors contributed to a toxic living situation that was not good for us. The boys and I would be starting over, just us. It was scary and exciting. We had never been on our own. I spent six months looking for an apartment, I was starting to think we would never find a place. Then there was a place.! It was perfect for the boys and me, with reasonable rent, and was in a quiet area. The night we moved, I realized that we were moving into an empty apartment, we did not have furniture, no stove, and no fridge. We had a couple of mattresses and our clothes. I panicked and called my mom, "Mom what am I doing, we have no furniture, it's going to be an empty apartment!" My mom said to me so gently, "Mija, when we moved into our apartment, we only had your crib and a mattress. You are going to be fine" I immediately felt better. We put the two mattresses we had in the living room and made it work. Little by little things started coming together. We soon got a stove, then a fridge, months later a couch, and lastly a kitchen table. It did take some time, but it all came together. More importantly, we were safe. We had a roof over our heads. My place soon became a holiday spot, we would have Thanksgiving,

Christmas, and New Year's here. My sister lived downstairs from me; my mom

was five minutes away. It was perfect. I enjoyed fixing up my place. It was ours.

Chapter 14: Then there was TikTok.

During COVID, many of us discovered TikTok. It was how we got through that time. The more time I spent on that app, the more addicted I became. I would go on there and create videos, I was shy though, I did not know what I was doing. But I was making connections. Some connections were a blessing and I still have those people in my life. Two years into it, I was completely invested in this app. I was becoming more confident and bolder. It was a fantasy world; I could dress up and be whoever I wanted to be. I lived for the compliments I would get from everyone who followed me. It became my life, and I entertained anyone that came into my inbox. I was seeking attention and validation, but if you looked closely enough you could see the emptiness. This was my escape. When I was not working or hanging out with the boys, I was creating videos and making all these social media friends. This was my new reality. I would buy outfits just for videos and the tighter the better. The ring lights, the wigs, the accessories took up all the space in my room. I became the Selena of TikTok, I loved and needed all the attention I was getting. I did not care if it was good or bad attention. I would spend my nights going live on the app with others and spend the whole night drinking and having a good old time. I wanted all the fame, all the titles, and all the attention. But at night when the day was over, when the camera was off and the show was over, I was alone, I was missing something. I was sad and wanted to be happy. How could I do that?

When would I be satisfied and tired of looking for someone to genuinely love me? I would be disappointed many times but still, I stayed right where I was. I compared myself and my life to everyone on social media, I wanted their life, or so I thought. I know firsthand what it is like to put on a smile and be screaming on the inside. I had no idea that TikTok would cause my next fall, but this fall brought me to my knees. It brought me to complete surrender.

Chapter 15: I fell.

Most of the time we meet Jesus on our knees when we are so broken and desperate. I can tell you that was true for me. While in the prime of my TikTok years, I met someone. He lived in another state, so I did not think much of it. He was charming and said all the right things. He was about eight years younger and was the bad boy on this app. Everyone wanted to be his special lady. You can imagine how I felt when he was in my inbox every day telling me how amazing I was. I almost felt unworthy of it. He can have anyone he wants right?! Our daily texts turned into daily conversations on the phone. He would always be drinking during our video chats and wanted me to join him, so I did. I started drinking every day, I wanted to impress him. After a couple of months, we decided to meet in person, and after some quick planning, I picked him up at the airport. I ignored all red flags and went through with this. I was excited and hopeful, but it was anything but an enjoyable experience. He was completely different in person. His drinking was excessive, his temper was more than I was comfortable with. With my background, this was not a good combination. The first time that I was forced to sleep on my couch should have sent me running for the hills, right? No, I accepted the apology a few days later. This is what I knew, I was familiar with this behavior. After he went back home, we continued with this internet relationship. I honestly do not know what made me continue this.

A couple of months later, he was back in my home. What the next few weeks or months would bring was not what I imagined. The drinking and smoking of weed seemed to get worse. His temper and disrespect were worse. He would get on social media and disrespect me. He did not work so I had to pay for everything, including his habits. When I first met him, I had managed to save eight thousand dollars. I always feared not being able to pay my rent and bills. So, I was doing my best to spend as little as possible. And it was working. With this man in my home, I could see my account dwindling.

I would pay for anything he asked for because I did not want to deal with his temper, and I feared him. Now when he was not drinking, he was sweet and we would go to the store, buy things for dinner, and cook together. But the minute he was "lit" he was loud, obnoxious, and mad. Every night before he passed out, he would call me a bunch of horrible names. Once again, I would go to sleep crying. I would stay up thinking of ways to get him to leave. I even told him that my mom was going to be moving in for a while. Nothing worked. I was working from home a few days a week, but how could I concentrate with him? He would wake up drinking and I would just sit in the living room listening to music and cry.

We would go live on TikTok, and I was not allowed to talk to guys while we were on live, and he was jealous. He was insecure and tried his best to hide it, but I could see right through him. He talked about marriage but that was not what I wanted. I wanted him to be out of my home. I remember going to work and not wanting to come home. I walked on eggshells in my own home. Why was I so afraid of this person? Well, I had experienced things in my past that had me fearful. He never put his hands on me, but I always feared that he would. I would send my boys to my brother's house because I did not want them around him. He would tell me that he was going to change and that we would be married. But day after day he was the same. He did not want to change; he was dealing with his own demons.

One day it got so bad that I told him that I no longer wanted him there. He would not budge, he just kept saying that he would be leaving but never did. One morning we got into a huge fight, he packed his bag and said that I needed to pay for his Uber to get him to a hotel until he got a ticket. I did not care how much it cost I wanted him out. I paid for an Uber, and he left that day. I still did not feel relieved, I would not until he was out of the city. For two days he would be threatening me, I called the police officers and they said there was nothing they could do if he had not touched me. He said if I wanted him gone, I needed to buy his plane ticket, I only had $300 in the bank and the ticket was $239. I was desperate, I just paid for it, I needed him away from me. He began with the threats again. I was a wreck at work, I did not know how I was going to pay my rent. He was calling my phone with different numbers, and I was going crazy. I was trying to work but I could not focus. His father was even calling me, telling me that he will pay my rent if I let him stay. I refused; I needed him gone. I tried working but I kept thinking about how I got myself in this situation again! I got on YouTube saw this video and clicked on it, and I heard the man say "No weapon formed against me shall prosper" I listened to that whole sermon, and it gave me some comfort and hope. Why was I living in such fear? Why had I done this to myself? Why did I turn so far away from God?

I walked home after work and began to reflect on my life. Reflecting on the last 10 years, the last year and I started to feel so grateful. When I got home, I began to pray I got on my knees and asked God to forgive me for what I had done, I told him that I needed him and that I needed a miracle. Soon this man was out of Chicago, which did not stop the threats though. He continued for an entire year, only he no longer got to me. There were so many things that happened but that would be a whole other book. Just know he was impossible and tried to do anything to scare me. I had a couple of friends who supported me financially to help me with my rent and phone bills. I will forever be grateful for that.

 God made a way, and often he will use a situation to bring you back to Him. I began reflecting on how I let all this happen, how I no longer had money in my account. I was like that lost sheep. He used his rod and pulled me back for the last time. This was it, no going back to that life, back to a life without Jesus. I would spend my days rebuilding my life, spiritually and financially. I stopped drinking

and tried to smile again. I needed to focus on being a mother to my kids. They had

so much, we all needed a Savior. I am grateful for those who helped me during this

time and the entire process. I am grateful the Lord once again saved me, he used

that for His good. There was a divine purpose. I would end up getting that scripture

I heard that day tattooed on my arm. I needed to see it every day. Thank you, Jesus.

Chapter 16: How do I let go?

I spoke a little bit about my real father in the beginning, he was a big part of who I would become in my life. It was quite surprising because he was not around and had no part in my upbringing. I grew up longing for the love of a father, to be daddy's girl. I remember being in fourth grade and hearing my friends talk about what they did with their dads over the weekend. I was so jealous, I wanted that so bad. So, like any jealous young girl, I decided to make up my own stories. I would tell my friends that my dad took me fishing and that we would go for breakfast and spend the entire day together. There was a time when I would believe myself as I said these things. As I grew up, I stopped the lies, I just accepted that I did not have a father. Difficult childhoods often lead to difficult adult lives. I was not an adult yet, but I was on the road to a life full of hardships and hurt. I would go around looking for love in all the wrong places, I would jump at any boy who showed the least bit of interest in me. I was so promiscuous and wanted all the attention. I would let myself get taken advantage of because I just wanted to feel loved and accepted. Even though I knew these boys cared nothing about me. I was ok with it; it was a temporary fix. Deep down I felt ashamed and already stained due to childhood trauma. I would stop and think about where my dad was, and why he did not want to be around me. My mom said that he loved me, yet he left me. The only connection I had to him was my grandmother, who was his mom. She lived in

Mexico and she and I began writing letters to each other. That quickly ended when she wrote to me and said she was not allowed to communicate with me anymore. That broke my heart. He did not love me or want anything to do with me. There was nothing I could do about the fact that I had to accept it. As I got older, I would get myself into these relationships that were not of love.

I wanted to be a part of something. I wanted to be loved. My first real relationship lasted 5 years and the result was my Isaiah. That relationship was not what I had hoped it would be. After it ended, I was looking for something to fill that void and entered a relationship that was full of toxicity and hurt. I accepted all of that because I did not know I deserved better. My self-esteem was low, I would take any love I could get. During that almost 10-year relationship, I would have moments where I would blame my real father, I was so mad that he was not around. In my head if he were around then I would not be going through this, if he were around to protect me then I would not have gotten hurt as a child. The longing for him turned into anger, I could never forgive him for leaving me. I imagined him going after the guy and after my step-grandfather for what they did to me. I imagined him going after M and telling him that he better start treating me with respect and be thankful for what he had in me. But most of all I would convince myself that if he were around, I would not have been stuck in this relationship. I was becoming more broken by the day. My worth no longer existed,

I had no business getting into that relationship, and I needed to heal. I put up with things that I should not have, and I failed to see that I belonged to the Highest. One day I was at church, and they were talking about forgiveness. The pastor said close your eyes and think of the person that you need to forgive. My father popped into my head, and I was crying uncontrollably. I needed to forgive him, but how could I? I needed to let go of that hurt; I just did not know how to do that. I needed to let go of all the hurt. I needed to forgive my father, the man who hurt me when I was seven, my step-grandfather, and any man after that. But I did not know how. How could I let go of the abuse and internal scars? I wanted them gone. When I was alone at night I would think of these things, I no longer wanted to harp on those things. I thought about the abortion and how I wish I could take back that day. It all still hurt so much.

Chapter 17: Do not waste your pain.

I went back to church, only it was different this time, I had one goal and that was to get close to God. All these years I had been trying and was unsuccessful because I got in my way. I made everything and everyone else my God. I decided I wanted to join groups this time, I needed to be surrounded by women of God. One night in the group the sister said, "Don't waste your pain" and I immediately felt something in my soul. We all have struggled so much in life and most of us do not get the privilege to see that the pain we went through had a purpose. As I got older, I realized that it was all for something. I can appreciate my struggles and trials. Little by little I could feel the hole that was in my heart be filled with the love of Jesus. I was on fire for God, I began reading the bible, and I joined another group that taught us how to read the bible. I stopped drinking, I was praying and talking to God more. God isolated me for quite some time, it was just me and him. So much was changing, I was changing, and I found myself truly smiling and not pretending. I was hungry for Jesus. I spent so much of my life away from my Savior, I needed all of Him. All these years I was this soul that needed a Savior, I needed Jesus. I did not know how much. We go through life experiencing all these different situations. At the time we have no idea why it is happening and become angry at God. In my case I did not trust God, I associated Him with men who have always hurt me. We also do not know what it means to have a relationship with

Christ. We do not know how to lay our burdens down and allow him to be the driver in our lives.

One day I was reading the word, and it suddenly came to me, everything is meant to give God glory, we go through trials, and He gets us out of them. The truth is God tests our faith through trials. Let us look at James 1:2, "Consider it pure joy, my brothers and sister, whenever you face trials of many kinds, because you know that the testing of your faith produces perseverance." I could no longer waste my pain; it was all for a divine purpose. We are to look at all the trials we go through with joy. We know something greater will come from it.

I was growing in my walk; my faith was growing. I was faithful to going to church and tithing, I was inserting myself into bible studies but there was something I was still missing. I just prayed for it. It was not a feeling of loneliness. I just wanted more, I wanted more of God, and wanted to know what my purpose was. The church I was going to was big, I wanted a mentor. I was seeking accountability. You can often get lost in such a big church, I only knew the names of the ladies I was in the group with, but we were not friends. There was no texting or checking to see how I was or if I had prayer requests. It was just me; I would continue going and letting God direct me. One day I asked someone, "how do I become a Disciple maker?" I wanted to bring others to Christ. Soon I had a mentor, she was exactly who I needed. She was fierce, bold and did everything for the glory of God. I became exposed to so much of the bible, her interpretations, her testimony, her life was all so encouraging. She knew she would have to set me free one day, I was growing and ready to take off. I would soon leave this church and find my home church! More to come on that. I will no longer waste my pain; I will rejoice in all trials that come my way and be full of thanksgiving.

Chapter 18: Becoming the Godly Wife

After my divorce, I never thought I would want ever to get married. But I was also genuinely happy and told the Lord that it was up to him, and I had opened my heart to receive whatever it was God had for me. I told God that I wanted a kingdom partner but when the time was right. I was working on my relationship with Christ, I was learning how to listen to God. One day at work, my colleagues started talking about how they met their partners. They said that they had met them on a dating app. They asked me if I would ever go on a dating app. I immediately dismissed that. I used to be on dating apps, and it never ended well.

One day I was home and decided to go and choose a dating app to try it out. I began to write a long bio so that guys knew what I was not tolerating. I was in search of a Godly man. I was on it for about a week, I was already getting tired of the messages that I was getting. It all seemed familiar. I did not want it. I had decided that I was going to get rid of the app. Then I received a message; it was very thorough and thoughtful. I thought, hmmm could this be a good one? I was skeptical. But I went and messaged this guy back, the conversation flowed, and we exchanged numbers. We talked until 5 am the next day. In the conversation I found out that he lived 10 minutes away from me, I passed by his house every day to take my kids to school. We shopped at the same stores; I feel like we were meant to bump into each other.

I needed a man of God, a man that will pray for me, and with me. A man who would worship with me and teach me about the bible. Someone who would allow me to dream big and support me in all the things that I want to accomplish. A man who cherished me and would love me the way I needed to be loved. This man was the one. I knew it was him because I did all I could to push him away. He was patient and stayed right where he needed to be.

I still had an ounce of fear that this would end up with me hurt again. But he was loving and consistent. It went from "my goodness this man won't budge" to "Lord, this is the man I want to spend my life with!" He was gentle with me yet so strong.

I felt safe with him. He listened to me; he loved God. One day as he was talking about his love for the Lord, I could not help but think "how beautiful" he looked at that moment. I knew that I did not want to go out for coffee with anyone ever again. He was my person. I never thought in a million years I would be talking to my future husband. But see, that is the beauty of life and trusting what God has planned for you.

Six months later we were married! It was the best day of my life. And if I had to do it all over again, I would not change anything. Yes, it seems crazy, but why wait? I knew he was my blessing, and he knew I was his. He is an answer to my mom's prayers, an answer to mine. I have never had someone treat me the way my husband does, I feel protected and loved. Not a day goes by when he is not letting me know that he loves me. He is so good with the kids too. He loves and corrects them. I never have to open a door because he will always open it for me. I am his queen. I never imagined that I would be married to my best friend. I did not know love could be so gentle.

I wish I could say that it was a smooth transition from dating to marriage. I will admit it was hard for me to fully trust his judgment and submit to him the way I needed to. I had been used to being the one in charge of my finances, the kids, and all other decisions. The first couple of months I could not wrap my head around the fact that I had a partner who wanted the best for me, and for my family. A man who would never intentionally hurt us was a foreign concept to me. We bumped heads and I found us just going through it. He felt that he could never make me happy, and that was a horrible feeling for him. I felt as if he would get tired of this and leave. It was evident that we both had to get used to the non-toxic type of relationship.

One of the benefits of building a community was that I had plenty of godly wives whom I could talk to about my issues and what I was feeling. It turns out that most of them understood what I was talking about. Submitting to your husband in the way you submit to God was difficult. I felt better because I knew I was not alone in this. I was blessed with advice and prayed over, and I felt the change, and he did too. I make a conscious decision every day to not only to love my husband the way that he needs me to, but to submit to him the way that I submit to my God. I ask the Lord to continue to transform me into an instrument of peace. If there is a decision that I see him making I take it right to God, and I know that if the decision is not right for us, God will take care of it. Every day the Lord transforms me into the Godly wife that I was meant to be. My job is to respect, love, and trust my husband, and to support him in any decisions that he makes for us and our family. Even if that means he picks ugly curtains, I honor his choices. I am to stand behind him when the kids need correction, and never go against him on how he handles that. I will uplift him and make sure he knows that he is the one God sent for me. It is my honor to serve my husband, it is my honor to submit to him the way that I submit to Christ.

Chapter 19: My New Son.

I had to go back to this and add my new son to my book. Israel is almost nineteen and I am grateful that I get to be in his life. When My husband and I started dating and he told me he had a 17-year-old son, I became nervous. It is not like he is a little kid, what if he did not like me. He is older, he has his own mind. The day I first met him we hit it off right away, we bonded over my Coach purse while waiting in the lobby at church. We have a great relationship; I love him just as if he were my own. Since Israel lost his mom when he was a baby, I want to always make sure he feels loved here, and that he is treated the same as the other boys. Before his dad and I got married, we would spend time getting to know each other. Once we combined our families and we started living together I appreciated his presence. I remember I would come home from a long day at work, and he could tell if something was wrong and ask me if I was ok. We can sit and talk for hours. We would talk about so many different things, my faith, healthy lifestyles, and life. He always listened to me and respected my thoughts. Christian and Joel love him, they latch on to him. He gives them attention and advice. I am grateful for that. Since he and Isaiah are so close in age, they hit it off right away. They are quite different but manage to get along perfectly. He blended right in with us. Israel is a determined individual; he has goals, and he is smart. I know that God has a plan for his life. Right now, he is rebelling and knows of God but has not given his life to Jesus. Something I am grateful for is that God willing, I will be here to see all his big lifetime events, just like with my kids. I missed all his life, but I am here now and cannot wait to see him get married and have the ten kids he wants to have. I believe that I will see him serving in the church alongside my husband and me. He will be out street preaching and winning souls for Jesus. I claim that in Jesus' name!

Chapter 20: Opening My Heart.

Being open to love again was something that I struggled with. I had been hurt in some type of way in all my relationships. I was convinced I should be alone. That changed when I met my husband. I remember one night I was talking to God, and I was like, "Lord, you bring me someone when the time is right, but you know that I am happy right now" It was so relieving to know that God was going to take care of that part. I had never been happy and content where I was in life. I did not know what it was like to not be in a relationship, I did not like being alone and was constantly searching for someone. But this was not the case anymore. I was trusting God.

When I met my husband, I was skeptical at first, I was not used to a man being so nice and so thoughtful. The last relationship I had been in was so toxic, full of lies and narcissism. That was the typical type of relationship I would find myself in. As I reflect on these past relationships, I spend more time crying than smiling or being happy. That is not how it is supposed to be. I did not love myself though or have the love of Jesus in me so of course this is what my life would be. I would allow these men to treat me the way that they did. I would experience every type of abuse and think that is what I would deal with for the rest of my life. I thought it was normal.

Before my husband came along, I realized who I was, I realized that I was worth loving. That I was the daughter of a King. That the Lord who created the heavens and the earth calls me chosen. That is what was different. I would no longer tolerate to be treated any other way. Where I was used to insults from men, he lifts me up, encourages me, and never stops telling me how grateful he was for me. There has never been a time where I felt unloved. And I do not think I ever will. I found my best friend. I opened my heart to him and trusted that he would never hurt me the way I was used to.

This is what the Lord does, he restores you so that you can receive all the things that are for you. If I did not have God, I would not have been able to heal from those relationships, I would still be carrying all that baggage. It would carry over to every other relationship I attempted to get into. The cycle would just continue, but Jesus comes to break chains, he comes to heal your soul and give you joy and peace. Psalms 147:3 says, "He heals up the brokenhearted and binds up their wounds." I cannot tell you how light I feel now that I have laid those burdens down at the feet of Jesus. Thank you, Jesus.

Chapter 21: Broken Chains

I no longer look back and wish things were different or think why did all that happen to me. I now look back and think, "Look at my God, look at all he has done!" It all had a divine purpose, that I did not understand, and you know what I had no business questioning God to begin with. He has delivered me from so many things, let us talk about some. Sexual immorality was a big one, I did not respect myself and allowed others to not respect me either. I had same-sex experiences and entertained all sorts of things. I had many sexual partners, all while being unmarried. I struggled for a long time with masturbation. I was addicted, any chance I got I was seeking pleasure. I remember starting this at an early age. I could not get enough; it was another temporary fix. Alcoholism and drug usage were also things that made me feel good for a brief time. I began drinking daily and just wanted my life to go away. Self-harm, I had many thoughts of not wanting to be here anymore. I wanted my life to be over. I entertained the thought of taking my life. I began cutting in high school and continued into my adult life. Idolatry, I made the world, social media, and food my idols. They were always put first in my life.

Anytime I needed to feel better I would get on social media to get some type of compliments and eat all the chocolate and fries I could. Food always controlled my life. I thought about it day and night, I would eat to make me feel better. I would hide it from people. My stomach became my idol. Depression and anxiety are other things I used to struggle with. I was not happy no matter what I did. I felt unworthy, I felt that everyone could see stains. My spiritual stains. I would cry for no reason, I felt alone and hopeless. It may be hard to believe but I cursed way too much. Every other word was an 'f' bomb. My grandmother used to constantly tell me about my bad mouth, but it was a part of me. Or so it seemed.

You hear the songs and people that say Jesus is a chain breaker. I am here to tell you that he is. All the things that I have mentioned he has delivered me from. Once I gave my life to Christ, I became a new creation. I wanted to be like Jesus, I wanted to live a holy life. Being like Jesus does not mean that I will not ever sin, we will fall short daily. But there is a significant difference now, I do not want to sin, I do not want to go against the commandments of God. Everything did not go away right that second, but my prayers to the Lord let him know that I needed him to free me of those things. To free me from addictions, from sexual immorality, from drunkenness, idolatry, depression, and self-harm. I cried out to Jesus, and he answered my prayers, he heard me...he heard my cries.

You can imagine how it felt when the lord answered my prayers, who was I? I did not feel worthy. It was extremely hard for me to trust the Lord. To trust that he had plans for me and that he loved me despite all the times I rejected him. He gave me so many chances that I did not deserve. I no longer needed the alcohol, I needed

God. I decided to leave social media for a little while and when I returned, I decided that all my platforms would be to exalt the Lord. It would be all about him. I finally had joy in my heart. I vowed to be celibate until God sent my kingdom partner. My life was now for Jesus. I lived for him and him alone. I could not explain how grateful I was for the life that I had. I restored my relationship with my kids and enjoyed the blessings of motherhood. My past no longer determined who I was, I was set free from bondage, sin, and oppression. We can all have this reality because Jesus broke the chains of sin and death through his resurrection. He laid down his life for me, for us.

Chapter 22: My New Life.

Many people think that once you follow Jesus your life is going to be perfect. I can assure you that is not the case. Let me tell you, going through trials with Jesus is different. Jesus did not promise that our life would be easy, but he did promise it would be worth it. We will lose family and friendships. After I surrendered my life to Jesus, he isolated me for a while. It was just me and him. At first, I didn't understand why I was losing people, but it soon became clear. Many people get offended by my new life, they think I am judgmental and that is ok. I am not called to worry about others and their opinions. I am called to do what Jesus commanded. One of my favorite scriptures is:

[1] *"Blessed are you when people insult you, persecute you, and falsely say all kinds of evil against you because of me. Rejoice and be glad, because great is your reward in heaven, for in the same way they persecuted the prophets who were before you."*

-Matthew 5:11 NIV

I am called to share the good news with everyone, whether they want to listen or not. I am called to be obedient to the Lord. I am called for such a time as this.

---

[1] *All scripture quoted is from the Holy Bible, New International Version, unless otherwise noted.*

I reflect on my life and all that the Lord has brought me out of, and I can't help but thank my God over and over. I see all the blessings, all the favor and love. I see how he does work out all things for good. My life is to bring him glory, my existence is to worship him. My new life revolves around my Jesus, my marriage is centered around him, my home is filled with the love of Jesus, the bible studies, the new friendships, the outreach events, serving in the kid's ministry, and being a bible college student is all about him. I spend my days worshipping, learning about who God is, and listening to his voice. Worrying about my future is a thing of my past life, my life is in God's hands, I have surrendered every one of my children to him, so I can rest assured that he will take care of them. I can be confident my God has me, that he will provide all that I need and more. Go has been so forgiving and gracious with me. He has given me not one, or 2 chances, he has given me so many chances to get it right. And when I was ready, he received me with open arms. He rescued me and said I didn't belong in hell. That is my Jesus.

I once did a podcast and I said that I would go through all the pain and heartache a million times over, why? Because it all brought me to Jesus. I would not be here if it were not for him, I would not have the job that I have, I would not have the joy that I have and I would not be healed the way that I am. He has redeemed me, filled every crack in my soul and forgiven every sin that kept me in bondage. That is my Jesus. Do not get me wrong, I still fall short daily, but I have a forgiving Father who knows my heart, he knows every hair on my head, every thought and his grace and mercies are new every morning. All I want to do is live for him, know him, and be more like him. Being more like Jesus will help me love others the way that I am supposed to. I will be the godly wife and mother that I am supposed to be. I will have that servant's heart that Jesus had. Every day I realize that I was made to worship, and my life is to give him glory.

Another thing that I do now for the kingdom is share the good news with anyone who will listen. Before Christ I did not know of things like evangelizing or being baptized in the Holy Spirit. Once I learned that I also could speak in tongues and talk to get on a mic and speak in truth to the lost and broken, I was in awe. My first time being out, and evangelizing was at this huge Chicago event that happens. It was also the same day that my husband and I were married. I could not think of a better place I would rather be then out telling others about Jesus. I was so nervous, I did not know what to expect, but I was surrounded by my new church, and they were all passionate about the Lord. I was even more nervous when I was asked to talk on the mic, I had no idea what I was going to say. I prayed and t spirit provided the words for me to speak. It was amazing. I knew God was pleased with me. Our church is such an active church, they are out evangelizing daily. Being out there with my husband and my church family is part of my life now. We are privileged to be able to speak about what the Lord has done for us, and more importantly we speak the truth. We are called to correct and rebuke.

I also have a group of women that I can go to anytime I need prayer, or some fellowship. My new life includes me being in bible college. I never imagined I would ever go to college, especially 24 years later. But here I am, studying God's word and learning more about him. I have come a long way, I pray that my children will remember all the prayers, the bible stories, the lessons when they get older. I cannot wait to see what the Lord has planned for me and my family. I know that what he has planned is greater than I can ever imagine. Our God is loving, and he wants to give his children good things.

I pray that whoever reads this is encouraged and that you are not defined by your past. Jesus comes and heals you from the inside out. I pray blessings for every individual who picks this book up. I pray for the peace and joy of God to overflow in you.

I love you all.